James Middleton

How a Love For Nature and Dogs Shaped His Life

Alicia A. Ferguson

All Rights Reserved

No part of this publication may be reproduced, distributed, or transmitted in any form or by any means, including photocopying, recording, or other electronic or mechanical methods, without the prior written permission of the publisher, except in the case of brief quotations embodied in critical reviews and certain other non-commercial uses permitted by copyright law.

Copyright © Alicia A. Ferguson 2024

Table of Contents

Introduction

Chapter 1

Chapter 2

Chapter 3

Chapter 4

Chapter 5

Chapter 6

Chapter 7

Chapter 8

Conclusion

Introduction

James Middleton is a man of many dimensions—an entrepreneur, a mental health advocate, a lover of nature, and a steadfast member of one of Britain's most well-known families. Yet, despite the public's fascination with the Middleton name, much of James's journey has remained untold. While his sisters, Catherine, Duchess of Cambridge, and Pippa Middleton, have lived their lives under the glare of the global spotlight, James has taken a different path. His story is one of quiet resilience, creative ambition, and a deep commitment to living authentically in a world that often demands perfection.

This book takes you beyond the headlines and tabloid photos to reveal the man behind the Middleton name—a man who has grappled with mental health struggles, built businesses from scratch and found solace in the simplicity of the countryside. In these pages, you will discover a James Middleton few have seen: the young boy who grew up in the serene landscapes of Berkshire, England, finding comfort in the outdoors and forming an unbreakable bond with his beloved dogs; the passionate entrepreneur who transformed his love for creativity into a series of bold business ventures; and the mental health advocate who courageously shared his battle with depression and anxiety to help others confront their own challenges.

James's life may have been touched by the royalty that surrounds his family, but it is his individual spirit that stands out. His entrepreneurial ventures, from Boomf's quirky personalized marshmallows to Ella & Co's natural dog food, reflect his inventive mind and desire to carve out a path of his own. His love for animals and the outdoors has been a guiding force, giving him a sense of grounding amidst the whirlwind of public attention. And perhaps most inspiring of all, his openness about his mental health struggles has shed light on an issue often shrouded in silence, particularly among men.

What makes James's story captivating is not simply the proximity to royalty or his business acumen, but his authenticity in a world that often values surface appearances. He has faced immense pressures—both personal and public—yet continues to navigate them with grace and a determination to stay true to himself. His journey is one of highs and lows, triumphs and setbacks, but through it all, James has remained steadfast in his beliefs, carving out a life that reflects his values.

This book invites you to step into James's world—not the world of flashing cameras and royal events, but the quieter, more intimate moments that have shaped him into the man he is today. From his early years growing up in Berkshire to his public advocacy for mental health, you will find a story that is both deeply personal and universally relatable. It is a story of resilience, creativity, and the unyielding pursuit of a life filled with purpose and passion.

As you turn these pages, you will see how James Middleton's journey is not just one of privilege or public attention, but one of forging a unique path, facing personal battles, and building something meaningful in a world that is constantly watching. Whether you are intrigued by his entrepreneurial ventures, his advocacy for mental health, or his relationships, James's story offers something for everyone—a reminder that no matter the circumstances, there is always room for growth, understanding, and a bit of self-compassion.

So, step into James's world—there is much to discover, and it's a journey worth taking.

Chapter 1

Early Life and Family Background

James Middleton was born into a warm, close-knit family in Berkshire, England, in April 1987. He grew up in Bucklebury, a tranquil rural community surrounded by rolling hills, woodlands, and open fields that offered a peaceful environment. It was here, in this picturesque part of England, that James developed a deep connection to nature and the outdoors, which would later play a significant role in shaping his love for animals, especially dogs. The natural beauty of the countryside fostered a sense of calm and stability for James, providing an escape from the pressures of the world, especially as his family's profile grew in the media.

The Middleton family's roots in Berkshire were marked by a strong sense of community and connection to the local area. James's parents, Michael and Carole Middleton, raised their three children — Kate, Pippa, and James — with an appreciation for the simple pleasures of rural life, while also ensuring that their children were exposed to opportunities that would allow them to thrive. The Middletons were a quintessential example of a hardworking, middle-class British family. Michael Middleton worked for British Airways as a flight dispatcher, while Carole Middleton, a former flight attendant, later became the entrepreneurial force behind the family's eventual rise to prominence.

In 1987, Carole founded Party Pieces, a business selling party supplies that began as a kitchen table project. The company's success was largely due to Carole's determination and creativity, growing from a small mail-order business to a flourishing company that became a household name in the UK. The success of Party Pieces not only provided the Middleton family with financial stability, but it also instilled in James and his sisters a strong sense of ambition, self-reliance, and the value of hard work. Watching his mother turn a small idea into a thriving business had a profound influence on James, shaping his own entrepreneurial spirit and desire to create something meaningful.

The entrepreneurial environment James grew up in left a lasting impression on him. It wasn't just the success of Party Pieces that mattered, but the effort, dedication, and teamwork that went into building it. The values of perseverance, creativity, and independence were central to the Middleton family dynamic. James learned from an early age the importance of innovation and resilience, traits that would serve him well in his future ventures. His mother's hands-on approach to business and her ability to balance family life with her career undoubtedly influenced James's own ideas about work and family. This entrepreneurial spirit would later manifest in his creation of several businesses, including Boomf and Ella & Co.

Growing up with two older sisters, Catherine (now Duchess of Cambridge) and Pippa, James was the youngest in a household full of strong personalities and close familial ties. The bond between the siblings was exceptionally close, and their supportive relationship was a hallmark of their upbringing. The Middletons were known for their strong family values, and James's relationship with his sisters was built on mutual respect, encouragement, and shared experiences. Whether they were attending Marlborough College or spending holidays together in Bucklebury, the Middleton siblings were inseparable.

James has often spoken about how his sisters were his role models. As the eldest, Kate was naturally protective and nurturing, while Pippa shared his sense of adventure and love for the outdoors. Together, they formed a tight-knit trio, bound by family loyalty and a shared sense of purpose. Even after Kate married Prince William in 2011 and entered the global spotlight as part of the British royal family, James remained steadfast in supporting his sister. Although he was inevitably thrust into the public eye alongside his family, James always sought to maintain a balance between his public persona and his private life, a balance that was made easier by the strong foundation of family unity that had been built during their years in Berkshire.

The Middleton family's rise to prominence did not alter their core values of togetherness and humility, qualities that James has continued to uphold throughout his life. His close relationship with Kate and Pippa, as well as the love and support of his parents, has remained a constant source of strength and identity for James, even as the media spotlight on his family grew. This sense of family has deeply shaped James's character and ambitions, providing him with the grounding and perspective needed to navigate the challenges of public life and the demands of entrepreneurship.

Chapter 2

Education and Personal Interests

James Middleton's academic journey was marked by experiences that not only honed his intellectual abilities but also nurtured his creativity, independence, and entrepreneurial spirit. His early education began at St. Andrew's School, Pangbourne, a prestigious co-educational prep school in Berkshire. At St. Andrew's, James exhibited an inquisitive mind and a deep curiosity about the world around him. The school, known for its nurturing environment and holistic approach to education, provided him with the ideal setting to explore a wide range of subjects and interests.

James was a naturally bright student, though he was less concerned with academic achievements in the traditional sense and more drawn to creative pursuits. He thrived in subjects that allowed him to express his creativity and think outside the box. His strengths at St. Andrew's included arts, literature, and science—areas where he could experiment and apply innovative thinking. From a young age,

James demonstrated an entrepreneurial flair, always looking for ways to turn ideas into tangible projects.

After completing his time at St. Andrew's, James went on to attend Marlborough College, one of the UK's most prestigious boarding schools, also attended by his sisters, Kate and Pippa. Marlborough College's emphasis on tradition, independence, and academic excellence shaped James during these critical formative years. The school is known for fostering a sense of self-reliance and ambition in its students, and James thrived in this environment. It was during his time at Marlborough that his creative and entrepreneurial talents truly began to flourish.

At Marlborough, James's interests extended beyond the classroom. He was heavily involved in extracurricular activities that reflected his love for nature and the outdoors. The college's expansive grounds and proximity to the countryside provided James with ample opportunities to pursue his passion for outdoor life. He became particularly interested in beekeeping, a hobby that would later become one of his defining passions. His fascination with bees and the intricate systems of nature helped develop his understanding of sustainability and responsibility. This early connection to nature would grow into a lifelong commitment to environmentalism and animal welfare.

James's love for the outdoors also played a significant role in his emotional well-being. Growing up in a family constantly in the public eye due to his sister Kate's marriage to Prince William, James found solace in the natural world. The countryside became a sanctuary for him, where he could retreat from the media spotlight and find peace. His passion for animals was a direct result of his deep connection to nature, and he later became known for his advocacy for animal care, especially through his work with his dogs and his support for various animal charities.

In addition to his love for nature, James's time at Marlborough also saw the development of his entrepreneurial spirit. Growing up with parents who had built a successful business from the ground up, he was naturally inclined to follow in their footsteps. His mother, Carole Middleton, had founded Party Pieces, a party supplies company that became a household name in the UK. Watching his mother's dedication and creative approach to business left a lasting impression on James. He admired her ability to transform a small idea into a thriving enterprise, and this inspired him to pursue his entrepreneurial ambitions.

By the time he left Marlborough, James had developed a strong sense of independence and a desire to create something of his own. His entrepreneurial spirit was further fueled by his creative nature, as he often came up with inventive ideas that could be turned into business ventures. While his academic path may not have been as traditionally focused as some of his peers, his experiences at both St. Andrew's and Marlborough laid the foundation for his future endeavors.

James's first major business venture came in the form of Boomf, a personalized marshmallow company. The idea was to allow customers to print their photos and messages on marshmallows, a concept that blended creativity with entrepreneurship. Though the venture faced its challenges, it was an example of James's innovative approach to business. His desire to create unique, experience-driven products reflected the entrepreneurial mindset he had developed from an early age.

Throughout his life, James has continuously sought ways to merge his love for nature, animals, and creativity with his business ventures. Whether through his beekeeping, his focus on eco-friendly practices, or his work with animals, James's passions have always informed his professional pursuits. His entrepreneurial journey is a testament to the values instilled in him during his formative years, where the influence of his family, his education, and his love for the outdoors all played integral roles in shaping the person he would become.

Chapter 3

Building an Entrepreneurial Career

James Middleton's academic journey began at St. Andrew's School, Pangbourne, a highly regarded preparatory school in Berkshire, England. Known for its nurturing environment and commitment to developing both intellectual and emotional intelligence, St. Andrew's provided James with the foundation he needed to explore his early interests. Although not traditionally academic, James was curious and imaginative, often more engaged in subjects that allowed him to exercise his creativity than those that required rote memorization. His passion for the outdoors, art, and science began to take root during these years, as he displayed a strong affinity for activities that let him interact with the natural world.

St. Andrew's, emphasizing holistic development, also encouraged James to develop leadership skills and a sense of responsibility, traits that would become key in his future entrepreneurial ventures. James thrived in this supportive and balanced environment, where academic pressure was paired with ample opportunities to explore his passions. He was particularly drawn to subjects that allowed for creativity and hands-on learning, such as art and science, where his innovative thinking could come to life.

After completing his time at St. Andrew's, James continued his education at Marlborough College, a prestigious boarding school in Wiltshire that significantly influenced his personal development. Marlborough College is known for its academic rigor and emphasis on independence, fostering both intellectual growth and a sense of self-reliance in its students. For James, it was the ideal environment to further explore his interests in nature, creativity, and entrepreneurship.

Marlborough's extensive grounds, which included woodlands and open fields, were a natural extension of the rural life James had enjoyed growing up in Berkshire. His time at Marlborough allowed him to deepen his connection to the countryside and cultivate his passion for nature. It was here that James's love for beekeeping first began to blossom. The school's setting provided ample opportunity for him to observe and learn about ecosystems, wildlife, and the intricate relationships between species, all of which fascinated him. Beekeeping became one of his primary hobbies, and it was through this that James learned important lessons about patience, care, and the value of working in harmony with nature—lessons that he would carry into his adult life.

James's passion for the outdoors extended beyond beekeeping. He loved the countryside and found peace in spending time with animals, especially dogs, which became a central part of his life. The solitude and serenity of rural life gave him a much-needed escape from the pressures associated with being part of the Middleton family, especially after his sister Kate's marriage to Prince William put the family under intense public scrutiny. The outdoors became a place of solace and fulfillment for James, allowing him to disconnect from the public eye and reconnect with himself. His strong connection to nature also inspired his work in mental health awareness, where he advocates for the therapeutic benefits of spending time outdoors and caring for animals.

During his time at Marlborough, James also began to develop his entrepreneurial mindset. Growing up in a household where entrepreneurship was valued—his mother, Carole Middleton, founded the successful party supplies business Party Pieces—James was naturally inspired to create something of his own. Watching the growth of Party Pieces, from a small business operating out of their home to a well-known company across the UK, had a profound effect on him. He admired his parents' ability to turn an idea into a thriving business, and their success ignited in him the desire to pursue his ventures.

Even as a student, James displayed a knack for thinking creatively and developing business ideas. He enjoyed the process of turning abstract concepts into tangible products or services, and his education at Marlborough further nurtured this entrepreneurial drive. The school's emphasis on independence allowed him to experiment with different ideas, from small ventures to collaborative projects with classmates. James was particularly drawn to the idea of creating something unique and experience-driven, reflecting both his creative mind and his desire to stand out in the business world.

After completing his education at Marlborough, James carried this entrepreneurial spirit with him into adulthood. He launched several businesses, including Boomf, a company that allowed customers to personalize marshmallows with their photographs and messages. Although Boomf faced its challenges, it was a clear reflection of James's innovative approach to business and his desire to merge creativity with entrepreneurship. His ventures also included Ella & Co, a dog food company inspired by his love for animals, further blending his passions with his professional aspirations.

James Middleton's academic journey at St. Andrew's and Marlborough College was instrumental in shaping both his personal interests and professional ambitions. It was during these formative years that he developed a deep love for nature, animals, and creative expression, as well as a strong entrepreneurial mindset. His education not only provided him with the skills needed to pursue his business ventures but also gave him the space to cultivate the passions that continue to define his life today.

Chapter 4

Life in the Public Eye

James Middleton's entrepreneurial journey took a creative turn when he founded Boomf in 2013, a company that offered personalized marshmallows printed with customer-supplied photographs or designs. The idea for Boomf came from James's desire to make gifting more personal and memorable. He noticed that the market for personalized gifts was growing, but many options lacked a sense of fun and novelty. This led him to the concept of merging technology with confectionery, resulting in an innovative product that was as Instagram-friendly as it was unique.

The inspiration for Boomf stemmed from James's belief that gifts should evoke joy and provide a lasting impression. He saw marshmallows as a playful canvas, allowing people to send messages, share memories, or unconventionally celebrate special occasions. The name "Boomf" was meant to capture the sound and excitement of something surprising and delightful, much like how the marshmallows would appear in the recipient's hands.

However, launching the business was not without its challenges. While the concept was original and eye-catching, turning it into a viable business required significant investment in technology and machinery. James had to develop a method that would allow high-quality images to be printed onto edible marshmallows while maintaining the product's taste and integrity. This required extensive research, innovation, and trial and error. He also faced the logistical hurdle of scaling the business and ensuring that the marshmallows could be produced efficiently enough to meet demand without sacrificing quality.

Despite these challenges, Boomf quickly gained traction, particularly among a younger, social media-savvy demographic. The product's quirky and shareable nature made it a hit on platforms like Instagram, where users would post photos of their personalized marshmallows, helping to drive organic marketing for the brand. Boomf capitalized on this trend, positioning itself as a fun, lighthearted gift option that was perfect for birthdays, holidays, and special events.

As Boomf grew, James expanded the company's product offerings beyond marshmallows. The brand started selling other personalized gifts, such as pop-out greeting cards and confetti-filled products, maintaining its emphasis on fun, interactive experiences. This diversification helped Boomf solidify its place in the personalized gift market, allowing the brand to evolve and stay relevant as consumer tastes shifted.

In addition to Boomf, James's entrepreneurial spirit led him to pursue other ventures, most notably Ella & Co, a dog food company named after his beloved cocker spaniel, Ella. Launched in 2020, Ella & Co was born from James's passion for animal welfare and his belief in providing pets with natural, healthy food options. As a lifelong dog lover, James was concerned about the highly processed ingredients found in many commercial dog foods. He wanted to offer an alternative that prioritized wellness and nutrition, using simple, wholesome ingredients to support dogs' overall health.

Ella & Co's product line focuses on natural, freeze-dried raw food that is convenient for pet owners but also nutritious for their pets. James's dedication to animal welfare is evident in the company's ethos, which emphasizes transparency, sustainability, and the well-being of pets. His passion for the outdoors and connection to animals influenced every aspect of the business, from product development to marketing. Through Ella & Co, James combined his entrepreneurial mindset with his love for dogs, creating a business that aligned with his values.

In addition to Boomf and Ella & Co, James has dabbled in other business ventures and investments, many of which reflect his creative approach to entrepreneurship. He has also been involved in mental health advocacy, particularly in promoting the benefits of nature and animal therapy. His personal experiences with mental health struggles have led him to use his platform and business success to raise awareness about the importance of wellness, both for people and animals.

Despite his successes, James has faced significant challenges and setbacks throughout his entrepreneurial career. Boomf, in particular, experienced financial struggles as it attempted to scale. While the brand gained a loyal following, the business had to navigate the complexities of production costs, marketing, and competition in a crowded personalized gift market. Boomf's reliance on social media-driven marketing also meant that trends could change quickly, and staying relevant required constant innovation.

Additionally, being part of the high-profile Middleton family meant that James's business ventures were often scrutinized by the media. Public perception of his businesses was sometimes colored by his association with royalty, which added pressure to his efforts to establish himself as a serious entrepreneur. There were times when Boomf faced criticism for being more of a novelty than a sustainable business model, and James had to work hard to prove that his ideas had long-term potential.

However, James has shown resilience in the face of these challenges. He has openly discussed the difficulties of entrepreneurship, from financial hurdles to the emotional toll of business setbacks. Yet, through it all, he has remained committed to his vision of creating meaningful, innovative products. His experiences with both success and failure have taught him valuable lessons in perseverance, creativity, and the importance of staying true to his passions.

Today, James Middleton continues to build on his entrepreneurial legacy, driven by a deep love for creativity, animals, and the joy of bringing people closer through personalized, thoughtful products. His story is one of resilience, innovation, and an unwavering belief in the power of simple, heartfelt gestures.

Chapter 5

When James Middleton's sister, Kate Middleton, married Prince William in 2011, his life, like that of the entire Middleton family, changed dramatically. The wedding of the future King of England and Kate, now the Duchess of Cambridge, captivated the world, instantly turning the Middleton family into public figures. As Kate's younger brother, James found himself thrust into the global spotlight—a position he never actively sought. Navigating this sudden fame required a delicate balance of maintaining his identity and privacy while handling the intense media attention that came with his new "royal-adjacent" status.

Before Kate's marriage to Prince William, the Middleton family had already enjoyed a certain level of media attention due to their successful business, Party Pieces, and their middle-class background. However, after the royal wedding, the media interest intensified to an unimaginable degree. The Middletons, including James, became subjects of relentless scrutiny, with paparazzi following their every move and tabloids speculating on their personal lives. Suddenly, James's private moments became public news, and maintaining a sense of normalcy was increasingly difficult.

In the face of this overwhelming attention, James worked hard to protect his privacy. He was frequently photographed at public events, especially when attending royal engagements or family gatherings. However, James was determined to carve out his path separate from the royal family. While his sisters, Kate and Pippa, often found themselves in the limelight, James made a conscious effort to stay out of it as much as possible. Unlike his sisters, he rarely gave interviews or made public appearances without cause, choosing instead to keep a lower profile.

One of the main challenges for James during this time was the impact the media had on his business ventures. His entrepreneurial efforts, particularly the launch of Boomf in 2013, were met with mixed reactions. Some saw Boomf as a creative and fun addition to the personalized gift market, while others dismissed it as a "celebrity-backed" business, attributing its success more to James's royal connections than to its actual merit. The fact that James was now part of the extended royal family colored public perception of his work, with some viewing him primarily through the lens of his association with royalty rather than as an independent entrepreneur.

The scrutiny also extended to his personal life. The media often speculated on James's romantic relationships and personal struggles. Reports on his love life were common tabloid fodder, and he frequently appeared in gossip columns alongside rumors and innuendos. This constant intrusion took a toll on James, who later opened up about his struggles with mental health, including depression and anxiety. In interviews, he candidly spoke about how the pressure of being in the public eye, combined with the demands of entrepreneurship, led him to seek professional help. His openness about these challenges humanized him in the public eye and showed a different side of the typically private younger brother of the Duchess of Cambridge.

Despite these challenges, James remained resilient. While media attention often focused on his connection to the royal family, James continued to emphasize his individuality. He made it clear that while he loved and supported his sister, Kate, his life was separate from the royal institution. His entrepreneurial ventures, including Boomf and Ella & Co, were testaments to his desire to build something of his own. His businesses were driven by his passions, particularly his love for creativity and animals, rather than a desire for fame or recognition.

James's relationship with the media also evolved. Initially reluctant to engage with the press, he gradually began using his platform to raise awareness for causes he cared about, particularly mental health and animal welfare. He became an advocate for speaking openly about mental health issues, sharing his personal experiences to help others who may be struggling. This marked a shift in how James interacted with the public, as he used his visibility not only to promote his businesses but also to contribute to important conversations about wellness and mental health.

Overall, the media attention that came with being Kate's brother undoubtedly altered the course of James Middleton's life. However, he navigated these changes with a clear sense of self, working to maintain his privacy and personal identity in the face of public scrutiny. While the world often saw him through the lens of royalty, James was determined to be seen for who he truly was: an entrepreneur, a mental health advocate, and someone deeply passionate about nature and animals. Through the highs and lows of media attention, he found a way to balance his public life with his personal values, staying true to himself amidst the challenges.

Chapter 6

Mental Health Advocacy

In 2019, James Middleton made the brave decision to publicly open up about his battle with depression and anxiety, a struggle that had plagued him for years. His decision to speak out about his mental health journey marked a significant turning point, not only in his life but also in the broader conversation around mental health, particularly among men. By sharing his story, James sought to normalize discussions surrounding mental health and challenge the stigmas that often prevent individuals from seeking help.

James revealed that his battle with depression began quietly, manifesting in feelings of deep sadness, hopelessness, and a sense of isolation despite being surrounded by family and friends. The emotional toll was overwhelming, leading him to retreat from social interactions and feel disconnected from the world around him. In interviews, he described how his depression made it difficult for him to get out of bed, face daily tasks, or feel any sense of joy or purpose. It was as though a "cloud" had enveloped his life, leaving him struggling to see a way forward.

The pressure of being in the public eye, exacerbated by his association with the royal family and the demands of running his own business, only intensified these feelings. James felt a deep sense of shame and guilt for not being able to "fix" himself, further isolating him in his pain. His mental health struggles also took a toll on his personal and professional life, affecting his relationships and his ability to manage his entrepreneurial ventures, such as Boomf, his personalized marshmallow company.

In 2017, after years of silently suffering, James reached a breaking point and decided to seek help. He turned to therapy, where he began to confront the underlying causes of his depression and anxiety. Additionally, he found solace in medication, which helped to regulate his emotions and give him the stability he needed to heal. James also credits his dogs, particularly his beloved black cocker spaniel Ella, for providing him with emotional support during this difficult period. He spoke candidly about how Ella could sense when he was struggling and would stay by his side, offering comfort and companionship in his darkest moments.

After finding his path to recovery, James felt a responsibility to use his platform to help others who might be struggling in silence. He understood the stigma surrounding mental health, particularly among men, and wanted to contribute to breaking down these barriers. In January 2019, James wrote an article for the *Daily Mail*, where he opened up about his experiences with depression, anxiety, and attention deficit disorder (ADD). In the article, he described the importance of seeking help and encouraged others to do the same. His honesty resonated with many, and his decision to speak out was widely praised for its vulnerability and courage.

James's mental health journey has since inspired him to become a passionate advocate for mental health awareness. He has aligned himself with various mental health charities and organizations, including Heads Together, a mental health campaign spearheaded by his sister, the Duchess of Cambridge, alongside Prince William and Prince Harry. Heads Together aims to normalize conversations around mental health and encourage people to seek help without shame or fear of judgment. James has supported the campaign by sharing his personal story and participating in public discussions on the importance of mental well-being.

In addition to his work with Heads Together, James has used his public platform to raise awareness about mental health through various public speaking engagements, interviews, and written articles. He has consistently emphasized the importance of speaking openly about mental health struggles and seeking support when needed. In particular, he has focused on addressing the unique challenges men face when it comes to mental health, including societal expectations to "tough it out" or suppress emotions. By speaking openly as a man who has faced depression and anxiety, James hopes to challenge these harmful norms and encourage men to be more vulnerable and proactive in caring for their mental well-being.

James's advocacy efforts also extend to his involvement in other mental health organizations. He has partnered with Pets As Therapy, a charity that provides animal-assisted therapy to people dealing with mental health issues. James's own experience with his dogs has fueled his belief in the healing power of animals, and he actively supports the organization's work to bring comfort and emotional support to those in need.

Through his public statements, partnerships with mental health organizations, and personal advocacy, James Middleton has become a strong voice in the fight to reduce the stigma surrounding mental health. His journey from suffering in silence to seeking help and becoming a mental health advocate has resonated with many, offering hope and encouragement to others who may be struggling. By using his platform to share his story, James continues to contribute to the ongoing conversation about mental health, reminding people that it is okay to not be okay—and that help is always available.

Chapter 7

Love and Marriage

James Middleton's relationship with Alizée Thevenet began serendipitously and charmingly, much like a scene from a romantic film. In 2018, James met Alizée at a private club in London. The story goes that Alizée, a French financial analyst, mistook James's dog Ella for someone else's, and approached the table to greet the adorable black cocker spaniel. What began as an innocent encounter over a shared love of dogs blossomed into a deep and meaningful relationship. James has often credited Ella with helping to break the ice, as his beloved companion played an essential role in their meeting.

Alizée, a woman of intellect and charm, quickly formed a bond with James. Despite their different backgrounds—James, a public figure in the UK due to his connection to the royal family, and Alizée, a more private individual with a career in finance—the two found common ground in their love of nature, animals, and a shared sense of adventure.

Their relationship was characterized by mutual respect and admiration, with each partner bringing out the best in the other. James, known for his love of the outdoors and entrepreneurial spirit, found in Alizée someone who complemented his passions with her deep-seated love for travel, the natural world, and animals.

As their relationship developed, it became clear that they shared strong values, particularly around family, privacy, and the importance of mental health. Alizée, who had lived in six countries before settling in London, shared James's appreciation for life beyond the spotlight, preferring quiet, intimate moments over the grandeur often associated with their public profiles. Together, they prioritized a life that was more grounded, spending time in nature, whether it was taking long walks with their dogs or retreating to the countryside. Their relationship grew in strength through these shared values, and Alizée provided James with a sense of stability and support, especially as he navigated life in the public eye.

In September 2021, James and Alizée sealed their bond in an intimate and private wedding ceremony held in the beautiful French village of Bormes-les-Mimosas. The wedding was a reflection of the couple's desire to keep their personal lives out of the public spotlight. Despite James's association with the royal family, the couple managed to keep the details of their nuptials under wraps, allowing them to celebrate their love in a private, low-key setting. The ceremony took place in a picturesque venue surrounded by close family and friends, including the Middletons and likely members of the royal family, though no official guest list was ever released. The couple's focus on privacy during this special moment in their lives was a testament to their shared desire for a quiet and grounded life, away from the pressures of the public eye.

James has described their wedding as a "beautiful" and "magical" day, filled with love and joy. The couple exchanged vows surrounded by the natural beauty of the French countryside, which echoed their shared love for nature and the outdoors. Alizée, who hails from France, was undoubtedly delighted to have their wedding in her home country, adding a personal touch to the celebration. The intimate nature of the ceremony allowed the couple to focus on the people and moments that mattered most to them, rather than the media attention that often follows James due to his familial ties.

Since their wedding, James and Alizée have continued to maintain a balance between their personal and public lives. While James's name is frequently in the headlines due to his connection to the British royal family, the couple has made a concerted effort to live a more private, peaceful life. They often retreat to their countryside home, where they live with their beloved dogs and spend time in nature. This lifestyle aligns with their shared values, allowing them to escape the hustle and bustle of public life and focus on what truly matters to them—family, health, and happiness.

James and Alizée's love for animals, particularly dogs, is another cornerstone of their relationship. The couple frequently posts pictures of their dogs on social media, sharing their joy in the simple pleasures of life—long walks, outdoor adventures, and quiet moments at home. Their shared love for their pets speaks to the deep bond they have, not only with each other but with the natural world around them.

In their marriage, James and Alizée have found a way to navigate the complexities of public life while staying true to their core values. Together, they have built a life centered around privacy, family, and a deep connection to nature, proving that even in the face of intense public scrutiny, it is possible to lead a fulfilling and balanced life. Their story is one of love, mutual respect, and a commitment to living authentically, away from the spotlight that so often follows them.

Chapter 8

Passion for Dogs and Animal Welfare

James Middleton's deep love for his dogs, especially his beloved cocker spaniel Ella, has been one of the most defining aspects of his life. Ella, who has been by his side for many years, is not just a pet to him—she has become a symbol of resilience, companionship, and unconditional love. James has frequently spoken about the role his dogs have played in his life, particularly during his battle with depression and anxiety. He credits Ella and his other dogs with helping him navigate through some of his darkest moments, providing him with emotional support and solace when he needed it the most.

Ella, along with James's other dogs, has been a constant presence in his life. In interviews and social media posts, James often refers to Ella as his "therapy dog," and he has openly discussed how her companionship helped him during his mental health struggles. Dogs, known for their intuitive ability to sense their owners' emotions, provided James with the comfort and grounding that he desperately needed during those tough times. The simple act of being around his dogs—whether it was taking them for walks in the countryside, playing with them, or simply being in their company—helped him focus on the present moment and find solace away from the public eye and the pressures of his life.

James's love for Ella and his other dogs extends beyond his personal life; it has also shaped his professional endeavors and advocacy for animal welfare. Over the years, he has become a vocal advocate for responsible pet ownership and animal welfare, using his platform to raise awareness about the importance of caring for animals and the positive impact they can have on people's lives. He has worked closely with animal charities and organizations that promote pet adoption, rescue efforts, and the overall well-being of animals.

One of the organizations James has supported is Pets as Therapy, a UK charity that provides therapeutic visits to hospitals, care homes, schools, and other establishments using trained therapy dogs. Given his own experience with how his dogs helped him manage his mental health, this charity's mission resonates deeply with James. He has taken part in several campaigns to promote the healing power of dogs and has spoken about how animals can offer emotional support to people dealing with mental health issues, loneliness, or trauma.

In 2020, James's love for dogs led him to a new entrepreneurial venture: the founding of Ella & Co, a dog food company named after his beloved cocker spaniel. The idea behind Ella & Co came from James's desire to provide healthy, natural food options for dogs, recognizing that what we feed our pets can have a significant impact on their health and well-being. The company focuses on offering high-quality, nutritionally balanced meals made from natural ingredients, designed to cater to the specific dietary needs of dogs.

The mission of Ella & Co goes beyond just selling dog food; it is rooted in James's passion for promoting a healthier lifestyle for pets. He believes that just as humans benefit from eating wholesome, nutritious foods, so do our pets. The company prides itself on transparency, with a commitment to using only the best ingredients and ensuring that all of its products are free from artificial additives or preservatives. As someone who has always been hands-on with his ventures, James is actively involved in the day-to-day operations of Ella & Co, from overseeing product development to engaging with customers and promoting the brand.

Since its launch, Ella & Co has grown steadily, attracting a loyal customer base of pet owners who are equally passionate about providing their dogs with the best possible nutrition. James's connection with his customers is personal, often sharing stories about his own dogs and their health journeys. His dedication to animal welfare is also reflected in the company's initiatives, such as supporting animal rescue organizations and promoting responsible pet ownership through educational content.

Through Ella & Co, James has not only channeled his love for dogs into a successful business but also into a platform that advocates for the well-being of pets everywhere. His hands-on approach, combined with his deep understanding of the bond between humans and animals, has helped make Ella & Co a brand that pet owners can trust. Additionally, his transparency and authenticity as the founder resonate with people who appreciate that the company is run by someone who genuinely cares about animals and their health.

In summary, James Middleton's love for his dogs, particularly Ella, has been a guiding force in his life. His dogs have provided him with emotional support during his battle with depression and have inspired him to become an advocate for animal welfare. Through his charitable work and the founding of Ella & Co, James has turned his passion for dogs into a mission to improve the lives of pets and their owners, promoting a healthier, happier lifestyle for all.

Conclusion

James Middleton's journey from a private individual to a public figure has been marked by personal challenges, entrepreneurial success, and a significant impact on mental health advocacy. As we reflect on his life and contributions, it is evident that James has left a lasting legacy that extends beyond his familial connections and business endeavors. His story is a testament to the power of resilience, the importance of mental health, and the potential for positive change through entrepreneurship.

James's courageous decision to publicly discuss his battle with depression and anxiety has had a profound impact on many, particularly young men who often face societal pressures to maintain a façade of strength and invulnerability. By sharing his struggles, James has helped to normalize conversations about mental health, offering a voice to those who may have felt isolated or reluctant to seek help. His openness has not only provided comfort to individuals facing similar challenges but has also encouraged a broader dialogue about mental health, breaking down stigmas and fostering a more supportive environment.

The influence of James's advocacy is evident in the growing awareness and acceptance of mental health issues. His work with mental health charities, such as the Heads Together campaign, has highlighted the importance of addressing mental well-being and has contributed to a cultural shift towards greater empathy and understanding. For many young men, James's story serves as a powerful reminder that vulnerability is not a weakness but a strength, and seeking help is a courageous step toward healing and self-care.

In addition to his contributions to mental health awareness, James's impact as an entrepreneur is equally noteworthy. His ventures, including Boomf and Ella & Co, have not only achieved commercial success but have also reflected a broader trend towards sustainability and personal branding. Boomf's innovative approach to personalized marshmallows captured the public's imagination, while Ella & Co represents a commitment to providing healthy, natural options for pets, aligning with a growing consumer preference for responsible and ethical products.

James's entrepreneurial endeavors are emblematic of a shift towards brands that emphasize authenticity, transparency, and sustainability. By creating businesses that reflect his values and passions, James has set a standard for how personal branding can be seamlessly integrated with entrepreneurial success. His hands-on approach, combined with a genuine dedication to his ventures, has helped to build brands that resonate with consumers on a personal level, contributing to the rise of a more conscious and connected marketplace.

The lasting impact of James Middleton's public discussion on mental health and his influence as an entrepreneur underscores a broader narrative of positive change. His willingness to share his journey has inspired many to confront their challenges with greater openness and compassion. Meanwhile, his business ventures have contributed to a growing trend of sustainability and personal branding, demonstrating that success can be achieved while staying true to one's values.

As we conclude this exploration of James's life and achievements, it is clear that his legacy is defined by more than just his public profile or business successes. His contributions to mental health advocacy, coupled with his innovative approach to entrepreneurship, have set a precedent for how personal experiences can drive meaningful change and inspire others. James Middleton's story is a reminder that personal struggles can lead to powerful advocacy and that entrepreneurship, when guided by authenticity and purpose, can make a lasting impact on society.

Printed in Great Britain
by Amazon